Anne's Amazing Alphabet Adventures

Las increíbles Aventuras de Anna su Alfabeto

ILLUSTRATIONS BY
Rubén Augusto Iglesias Segrera

CHERYL ANNE

Book Publishers Network
P. O. Box 2256
Bothell, WA 98041
425-483-3040
www.bookpublishersnetwork.com

Copyright 2017 © Cheryl Anne
Illustrations by Rubén Augusto Iglesias Segrera

10 9 8 7 6 5 4 3 2 1

ISBN   978-1-945271-26-7
LCCN   2016958081

DEDICATION

This book is dedicated to all the children who love to read.

ACKNOWLEDGMENTS

I am so thankful for my very best friend, Ken Marcum. I love you for always pushing me to continue working on making my dreams come true. I could never have done this without all your love and support.

Thank you to Julieta and Pat Crosby. You believed in me and my adventure and introduced me to the most amazing man, Rubén Segrera, the illustrator of my books. I am so happy that he is my mascot robot in all my amazing adventures. You have given my stories life more than I ever imagined. I love you. Thank you so much.

Thank you also to Stephen Plowman for all your help to make me a children's book author.

I thank my children, Jake and Tammy, Justin and Amanda, and Allison and Seth and my grandchildren Landon, Alyssa, and Laney. This is all for you, because of you.

And thank you to all my friends who continue to give me inspiration and love my funny stories.

LETTER A

Letra A

ALYSSA AND AMANDA

Alyssa y Amanda

SOUTH
AMERICAN

N
W   E
S

2

AFRICA

Alyssa and Amanda are army ants. Alyssa and Amanda live in Africa.

Alyssa y Amanda son unas hormigas del Ejército. Alyssa y Amanda viven en Africa.

4

5

They have agreed to accept a top secret assignment, a very important rescue mission, and are on their way to the airport.

Ellas han acordado aceptar una misión clasificada ultra secreta, una misión de rescate muy importante y están en camino al aeropuerto.

After they board the airplane, their orders are to fly to Argentina, South America.

Después de que abordan el avión, tienen órdenes para volar a Argentina en Sudamérica.

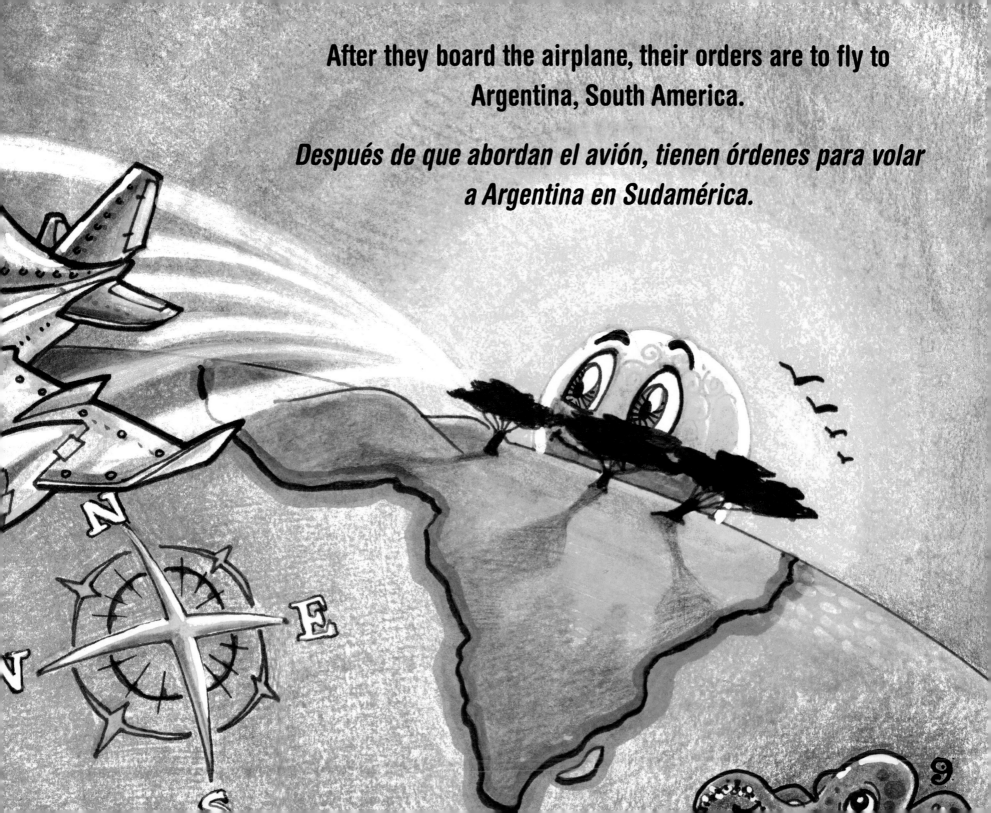

This is going to be quite an adventure. Now they are in a jeep heading for another airfield in the jungle.

Esta va a ser toda una aventura. Ahora están en un jeep en dirección a otra pista de aterrizaje en la selva.

Once there, they hop into a giant hot-air balloon.

Una vez allí saltan en un globo aerostático gigante.

12

13

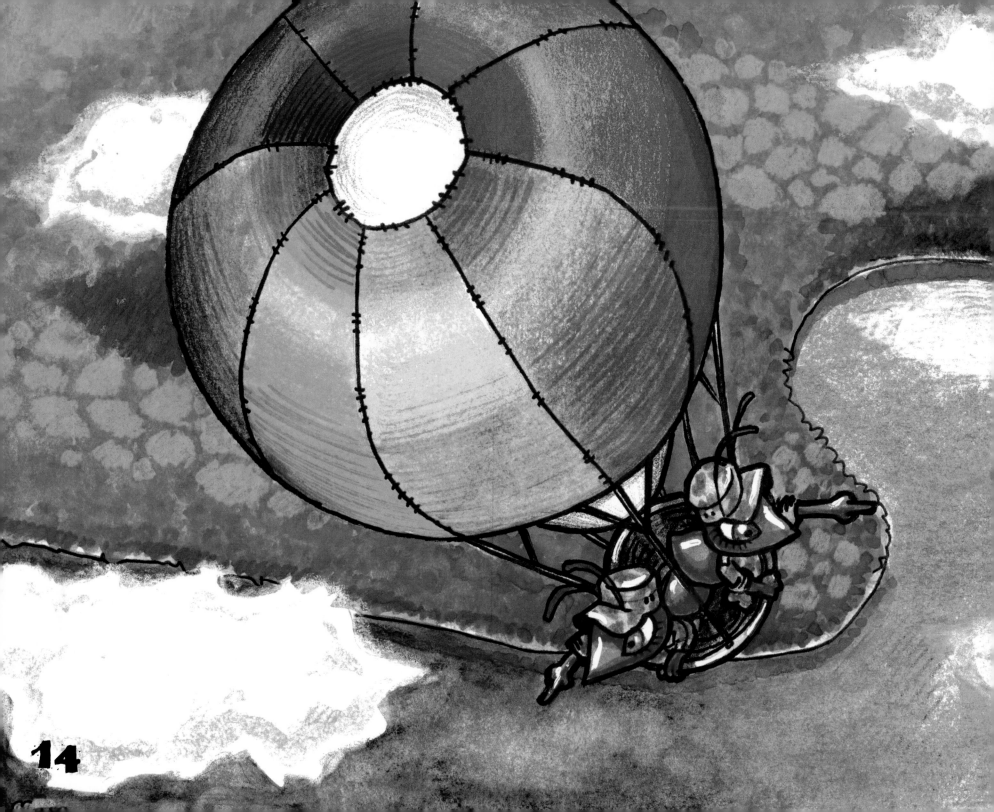

They soar across the country heading to the largest river in the world, the Amazon.

Se elevan por todo el país en dirección al río más grande del mundo El Amazonas.

15

After they arrive and land, they meet Alli. She is an alligator and special agent for the army. She will be taking them to the river where an airboat is waiting.

Después de que llegaron y aterrizaron se reúnen con Alli, ella es un cocodrilo y es agente especial para el Ejército. Ella las llevará al río, donde un bote de aire está esperándolas.

Alli aims the boat down the river. This is an amazing ride. They are amused by the apes ascending into the trees along the way.

Alli dirige el bote siguiendo la corriente del rio. Es un paseo increíble. Estaban muy entretenidos con los gorilas que se subían a los arboles a través del camino.

They are given their final orders—all together, they must
find Andrea, a missing anaconda.

*Se les dio las ordenes finales, realmente necesitan
encontrar a Andrea, una anaconda que está perdida.*

21

Andrea has been admired by all for her achievements as a famous anthropologist in the Amazon Jungle searching for a rare plant that grows high in the treetops that may be an antidote for arthritis.

Andrea ha sido admirada por todos sus logros como una arqueóloga famosa en la Selva de las Amazonas por la búsqueda de una planta rara que crece en lo alto en las copas de los árboles que puede ser usado como antídoto para la artritis.

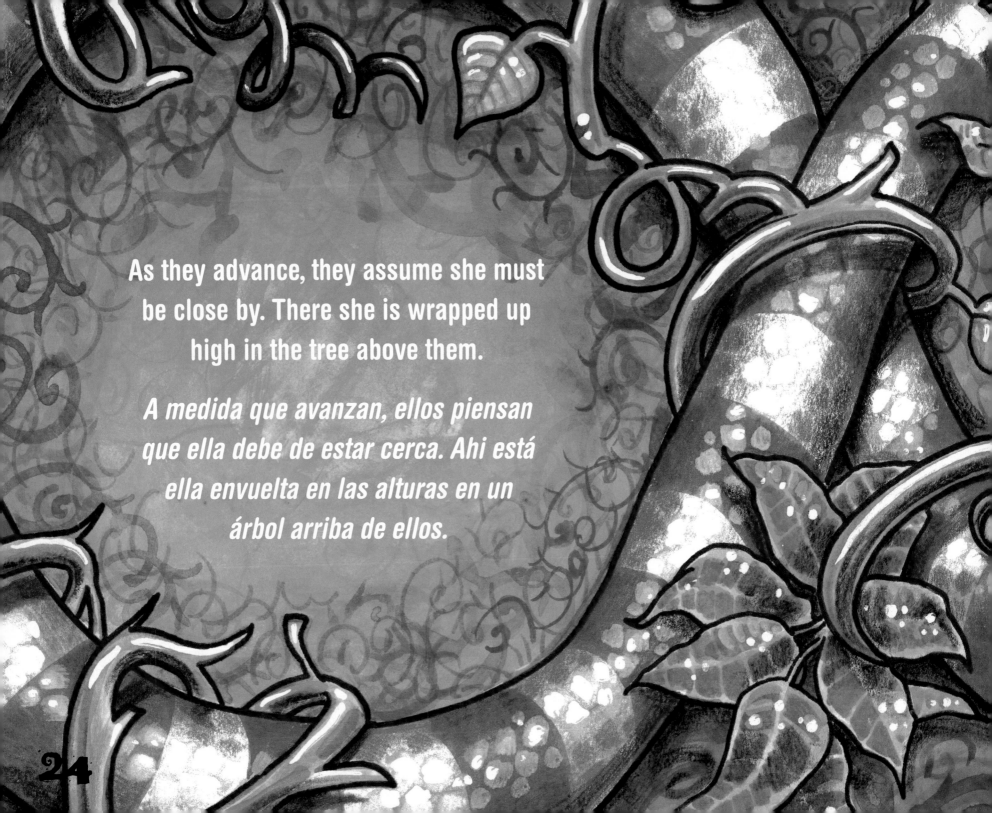

As they advance, they assume she must be close by. There she is wrapped up high in the tree above them.

A medida que avanzan, ellos piensan que ella debe de estar cerca. Ahi está ella envuelta en las alturas en un árbol arriba de ellos.

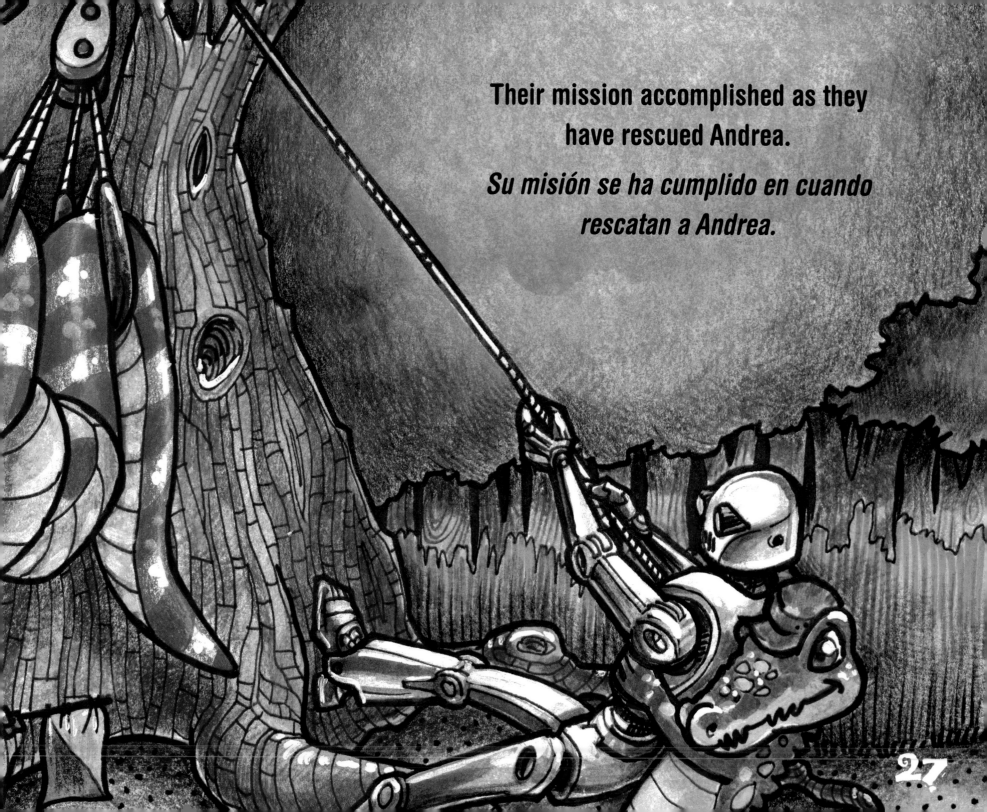

Their mission accomplished as they
have rescued Andrea.

*Su misión se ha cumplido en cuando
rescatan a Andrea.*

27

Letter B

Letra B

Billy and Bobbie Bats

Los murciélagos de Billy y Bobbie

BAHAMAS

N

W   E

S

Billy and Bobbie live on a big bright blue boat
in the Bahamas.

*Billy y Bobbie viven en un Bote Brillante
grande y azul en las Bahamas.*

Billy and Bobbie are brothers and best friends.

Billy y Bobbie son hermanos y mejores amigos.

Today is their birthday so they are picking up their buddies Barbara and Betty and taking them to the beach for a barbecue.

Hoy es su cumpleaños así que van a recoger a sus amigas Bárbara y Betty y los van a llevar a la playa a una parrillada.

Betty and Barbara are also bringing
along their baby bats.

*Betty y Bárbara van a traer también sus
bebes murciélagos.*

40

The girls have brought along a basket full of burgers, buns, and baked beans.

Las muchachas van a traer una canasta llena de panecillos para hamburguesas y frijoles horneados.

At the beach, the baby bats blow up balloons for the party while Billy and Bobbie start the barbecue.

En la playa los bebes murciélagos inflan globos para la fiesta mientras que Billy y Bobbie empiezan la parrillada.

The girls are putting on their bathing suits so they can help the baby bats build a sandcastle and play with their beach ball.

Las muchachas se pones su trajes de baño para poder ayudar a los bebes murciélagos a construir un castillo de arena y jugar con una pelota de playa.

The girls surprise the boys with brand-new bikes
with big bows.

*Las muchachas sorprenden a los muchachos con unas
bicicletas nuevecitas con unos moñosgrandiosos.*

All together, they sing
Happy Birthday and enjoy the
boys' favorite banana cake.

*En conjunto ellos cantan Feliz
Cumpleaños y disfrutan el pastel de
plátano, el favorito de los muchachos.*

49

ABOUT THE AUTHOR

Born and raised in Napa, California, Cheryl Anne now lives in Washington State with her boyfriend, Ken, and their two cats, Koo-Koo and Prudence. She has always loved reading books, writing stories, and sharing her writings with family and friends. Her three wonderful children and three awesome grandchildren live close by, so she can visit them often.